We Love Yom Kippur

Honor Head

WAYLAND

First published in Great Britain in 2007 by
Wayland, an imprint of Hachette Children's Books

Hachette Children's Books
338 Euston Road, London NW1 3BH

Produced for Wayland by Q2A Media
Editor: Jean Coppendale
Senior Design Manager: Simmi Sikka
Designer: Sheeba Narain
Consultants: Jane Clements and Rachel Montague from
the Council of Christians and Jews

A catalogue record for this book is available from
the British Library.

ISBN 978 0 7502 5257 7

Printed in China

Wayland is a division of Hachette Children's Books, an
Hachette Livre UK company.

The publishers would like to thank the following for
allowing us to reproduce their pictures in this book:

Shutterstock: title, 9 Lisa F. Young / Alamy: 4, Profimedia
International s.r.o. / REUTERS: 5, Michael Dalder; 23,
Havakuk Levison / CORBIS: 6, PoodlesRock; 7,
Bettmann; 11, Ted Spiegel; 12, Steve Raymer; 14, Philippe
Lissac/Godong; 15, David Rubinger; 17, Karen Huntt /
Photolibrary: 8, Foodpix; cover, 13, 19, Photo Researchers,
Inc.; 16, The Bridgeman Art Library / Lily & Rob: 10 /
Ark Religion: 18, Helene Rogers / Shutterstock: 20, Blaz
Kure / Judy Lash Balint: 21 / Sigalit Perkol: 22.

Contents

What is Yom Kippur? 4

Moses and the golden calf 6

The eve of Yom Kippur 8

Special blessings 10

At the synagogue 12

Prayers for forgiveness 14

Jonah and the whale 16

All is forgiven 18

Fasting 20

The festival of bicycles 22

Index and glossary 24

What is Yom Kippur?

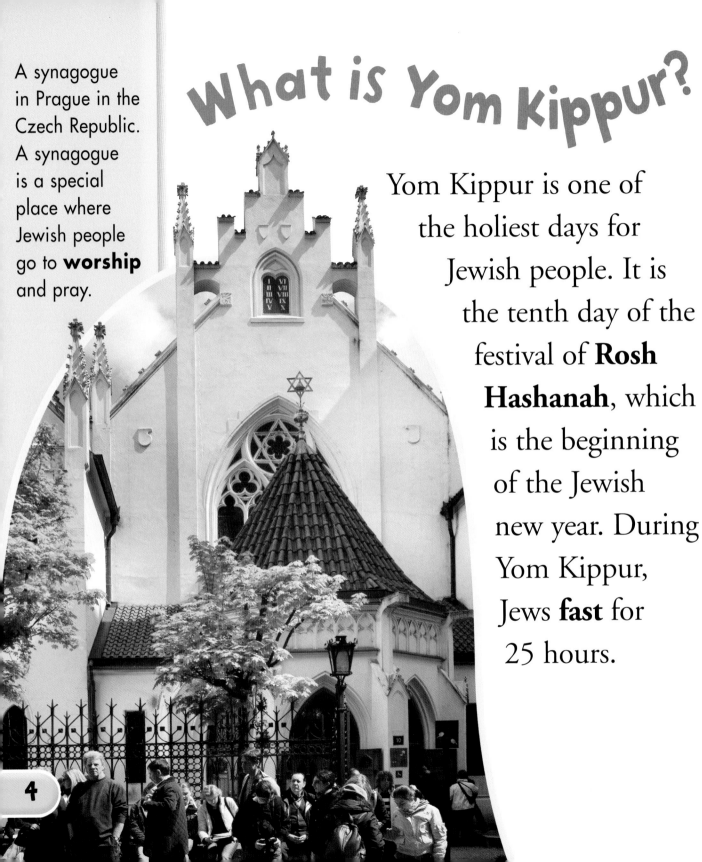

A synagogue in Prague in the Czech Republic. A synagogue is a special place where Jewish people go to **worship** and pray.

Yom Kippur is one of the holiest days for Jewish people. It is the tenth day of the festival of **Rosh Hashanah**, which is the beginning of the Jewish new year. During Yom Kippur, Jews **fast** for 25 hours.

Many Jews spend the day of Yom Kippur in the synagogue. They pray and ask God for forgiveness for all the wrong things they have done. They also remember how much God loves them.

The white kittel is only worn by married men as in this picture.

DID YOU KNOW?

On special occasions, such as Yom Kippur, many Jewish men wear a white garment called a kittel, which stands for pure thoughts.

Moses and the golden calf

God was angry when he saw the people of Israel worshipping a golden calf.

Yom Kippur began in **ancient** times with the **prophet** Moses. He found the people of Israel worshipping a statue of a golden calf instead of God. Moses pleaded with God to forgive them.

The people also asked God for forgiveness and fasted from sunset to sunrise. God forgave them and Moses said that from that day onwards, on the tenth day of the seventh month, the people of Israel would fast and ask God for forgiveness for their sins.

Moses went to the top of Mount Sinai and asked God to forgive the people of Israel.

The eve of Yom Kippur

Kreplach are small parcels of pasta filled with minced meat.

On the evening before Yom Kippur, many Jewish families pray to God. Then they have their last meal before they fast. The meal may include chicken soup with kreplach.

The meal may also include a bread called challah. This is a **traditional** Jewish bread, which is eaten on most holidays and festivals.

Challah is made from long strips of dough which are plaited together.

9

special blessings

Also on the eve of Yom Kippur, two special candles are lit to remember parents who have died. The candles are left to burn throughout the day.

The family lights two candles at the start of Yom Kippur.

10

Before they leave for the synagogue, many parents say a **blessing** for their children. The parents ask God to look after their children and keep them safe.

Many Jewish parents say sorry for the times they may have upset their children during the year.

At the Synagogue

The first prayer said at the start of the first evening service in the synagogue is called Kol Nidre. This is when Jews ask for forgiveness for promises they have not kept during the past year.

Men wear a tallitot, or prayer shawl, to say Kol Nidre.

Part of the
service at
the synagogue
on Yom Kippur
is reading the Torah.
The Torah contains all the laws
that God wants the Jews to follow.

No one can touch the Torah in case they damage it. So Jews use a pointer called a yad to follow the words.

Prayers for forgiveness

An important part of Yom Kippur is Avodah. This is a special service when Jews say a series of prayers to God to ask for his forgiveness.

The inside of a synagogue is brightly lit during services.

The **rabbi** leads the Avodah prayers. The first prayer is called Hineini, which means 'Here I am'. It reminds Jews that they have all done wrong things and all need forgiveness, even the person leading the prayers.

A rabbi is a Jewish leader. This rabbi is taking the special Avodah service in a synagogue in Israel.

15

Jonah and the whale

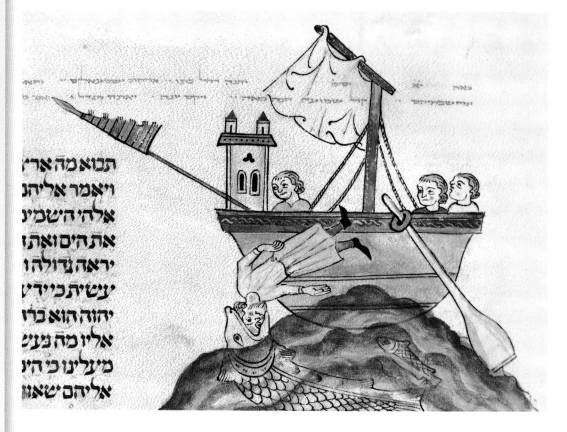

תבואמהאר
ויאמראליהנ
אלהיהשמינ
אתהיםואתז
יראהגדולהו
ינטיתכיידע
יהוההואברו
אליומהמעע
מעלינוכיהינ
אליהםשאנ

This picture is from a Jewish Bible. It shows that God sent a whale to save Jonah from drowning when he fell into the sea.

In the afternoon, the story of Jonah and the whale is read. God asked Jonah to visit some bad people and make them good. But Jonah wanted them punished, so he ignored God and ran away to sea.

While he was at sea, Jonah was swallowed by a whale. Inside the whale, he prayed to God for forgiveness for disobeying him, and God saved him. This story tells people they cannot run away from the bad things they have done and that, if they say sorry, God will forgive them.

This old wall painting from Turkey shows Jonah after three days, when the whale spat him out on to dry land.

All is forgiven

The doors of the Ark are open to show that the gates of heaven are open when prayers are said.

The synagogue services begin in the morning. Then there is a short break, and the afternoon and evening prayers are said.

18

DID YOU KNOW?

The Ark is a special cupboard in the synagogue where the holy Torah scrolls are kept.

The final prayer is called the Ne'ilah, which is only said on the day of Yom Kippur. Jews hope that God will forgive them as they stand and say prayers, and then hear the shofar, or ram's horn.

The long shofar note, which is blown in all synagogues at the end of Yom Kippur, is the final call for forgiveness.

19

Fasting

On the day of Yom Kippur, many Jews fast for 25 hours. This means that no one can drink or eat anything. This is so that people can pray and think about God, without having to worry about food. Children under the age of 13 and people who are ill do not have to fast.

Jews are not supposed to go to school or work on Yom Kippur.

On this day people are not allowed to have a bath, wear perfume or make-up, or wear leather shoes.

This sign says, "Fabric shoes for Yom Kippur". Leather shoes are not to be worn as they are a **luxury**.

21

The festival of bicycles

During Yom Kippur people in Israel walk and cycle along the wide roads.

In Israel, Yom Kippur is also called the 'festival of bicycles'. Israel is a Jewish country so most Jews do not drive their cars during Yom Kippur.

Children play
safely on the
roads in Israel
on Yom Kippur,
as there is
no traffic.

Children enjoy riding their bicycles
on the empty roads. They also go
roller-skating and skateboarding.

Index and glossary

A
Ark 14, 19
Avodah 14, 15

B
blessing 11, 24

C
candles 10
challah 8, 9

F
forgiveness 5, 7, 12, 14, 15, 17, 19

G
golden calf 6

I
Israel 6, 7, 21, 22, 23

J
Jonah 16, 17

K
kittel 5
Kol Nidre 12, 18, 19
Kreplach 8

M
Moses 6, 7
Mount Sinai 7

N
Ne'ilah 19

P
prophet 6, 24

R
rabbi 13, 15, 24

roller-skating 23
Rosh Hashanah 4, 24

S
shofar 13
sins 7
skateboarding 23
synagogue 4, 5, 11, 12, 13, 18, 19

T
Torah 13, 14, 18

W
whale 16, 17
worship 4, 6, 24

Y
yad 12

ancient a very long time ago

blessing to ask God to look after someone

fast to go without food or drink

luxury something which costs a lot of money and which you don't really need

prophet someone who teaches the word of God on Earth

rabbi a Jewish religious leader

Rosh Hashanah the Jewish New Year

traditional something passed down from generation to generation

worship to show love and respect to God